OVERCOMING DEPRESSION

The Essential Guide to Sustaining Relief from Depression

S.E. Charles

DEDICATION

This book is dedicated to those in search of essential information and practical skills to help manage and control their struggle with depression.

CONTENTS

INTRODUCTION

Depression is a mood disorder that involves persistent and intense feeling of sadness, low mood, and loss of interest. It is capable of making you feel worthless.

Most often we think that depression is just a case of extreme sadness. When we are faced with a tragedy, we feel depressed. But after a while it goes away. That's what the general belief is. But depression is far more than a mere bout of sadness. It is something with the potential to cause extreme harm and ruin lives, if not treated appropriately.

This is a pretty common psychological disorder. If you are currently battling it, know that you have company. Millions of people are suffering from this issue across the world. It is the most common illness in the world, according to the World Health Organization (WHO). It affects an estimated 350 million people worldwide.

In this insightful guide, you will find useful techniques, essential information and practical skills to help you manage and control your struggle with depression

CHAPTER 1 – OVERVIEW AND CAUSES OF DEPRESSION

In modern society, depression is a big problem. It is one issue that can throw the lives of not only the individuals affected out of balance, but also those of their loved ones. And it gets more disturbing to learn that more and more people are falling into it.

What is Depression?

Depression is a mood disorder that involves persistent and intense feeling of sadness, low mood, and loss of interest. It is capable of making you feel worthless.

The illness produces negative effects on the way you think, act and feel - your response to life generally. It usually makes activities that you loved engaging in become uninteresting.

It is not unusual to become depressed every now and

then. Certain events in life can cause a person to have feel pretty low. But if these are not promptly dealt with, they could lead to clinical issues.

The disorder is suspected if you experience the unpleasant feelings that last for at least two weeks. It is especially likely when these symptoms get in the way of your regular daily activities.

This is a pretty common psychological disorder. If you are currently battling it, know that you have company. Millions of people are suffering from this issue across the world.

It is the most common illness in the world, according to the World Health Organization (WHO). It affects an estimated 350 million people worldwide.

In any two-week period, about 7.6 percent of people who are older than 12 years suffer from depression, as reported by the Centers for Disease Control and Prevention (CDC).

Another estimate claims that up to 15 percent of the general population will experience clinical depression at some point during their lifetime.

What Depression is not

Yes, this mood disorder comes with feelings of sadness. But do not confuse it with sadness or grief.

Certain challenges that people experience in the course of their everyday life can cause sadness or grief. For example, the loss of a loved one could cause these feelings. Loss of job and end of a romantic relationship can also lead to same.

It's common to hear people experiencing such challenges saying they are depressed. But the feelings are merely normal responses to unsettling life events. They are not necessarily signs of clinical depression.

Normally, you should get over these symptoms after a few days.

A clinical disorder can only be suspected when they persist for longer than the length of time that is considered normal.

Forms of Depression

There are many ways in which a person may experience this psychological illness. They typically differ in terms of what leads to their development.

Here are some of the common forms of depression:

Postpartum depression

After they have given birth, many women suffer from acute depression which is commonly known as postpartum or postnatal depression. Because of the hormonal changes that occur in the body during pregnancy, these symptoms are often triggered

Some might consider it same as the so-called "baby blues." But postpartum or postnatal depression is more serious than that. Baby blues are considered to be common among mothers. They may have trouble sleeping, feel anxious at times, have mood swings, episodes of crying or may have loss of appetite.

Women with this disorder do not just have mild

depressive symptoms. With postpartum depression, symptoms are very severe and last much longer. They experience major, full developed depression either during pregnancy or after delivery. It presents symptoms that make it extremely hard for the women to take care of themselves or their babies.

Bipolar disorder or depression

This is not entirely depression, but its symptoms are part of the manifestations. Formerly known as manic depression, bipolar disorder is characterized by episodes of mania and depression, with periods of normal mood in-between. Mania is characterized by a feeling of euphoria in which the individual has elaborate ideas, displays unlimited energy, needs little sleep, and exhibits great self-assurance. While in a manic state people's thoughts race, they speak too fast, and they demonstrate poor judgment. A person with this disorder may feel euphoric or highly excited at a time and in very low mood at another.

Although it can occur at any age in a person's life, bipolar disorder often happens during late adolescent years and often appear as depression during the teenage years. Researchers estimate that people with this condition are depressed about 40 percent of the time.

Dysthymia

Dysthymia is characterized as a depressive disorder that is less severe than major depression. It is often characterized as chronic depression. Also called persistent depressive disorder, this is a form that exhibits depressive symptoms for a period of at least two years.

People with dysthymia usually eat too little or too much. But the dictating part about dysthymia is feeling blue, or depressed. Although dysthymia sufferers do not live with severe depression, it is more chronic and can affect your life negatively by keeping you from being productive and enjoying yourself.

A person with dysthymia experiences episodes of major depression as well as episodes of less critical symptoms.

Major depressive disorder with seasonal pattern

This was previously known as seasonal affective disorder (SAD). is a type of depression which occurs periodically and relates with changes in the seasons. There are two types of SAD. The most common is referred to as Winter Depression. It is a form that typically affects people during winter months. Those living in areas with very harsh or long winters are mostly affected These symptoms begin in late fall or early winter.

The second, and less common form of SAD, is summer depression. A person dealing with summer depression would begin to experience symptoms in spring, and the symptoms would stop in fall.

It is estimated that about 5 percent of the population experience some time of SAD. It typically affects those in their early 20s and is less likely to develop as your age increases. Of those affected with the disorder, women outnumber men four to one.

Psychotic depression

This form also goes under the name major depressive

disorder with psychosis.

Along with the usual symptoms of depression, Psychotic depression is a mental disease that is a mix of depression and psychosis. It occurs when a person displays both severe depression and a break with reality. It involves aspects of psychosis that can manifest into irrational behavior. The loss of contact with reality may take the form of delusions, hallucinations or thought disorders. Those suffering from psychotic depression often believe that their thoughts are not their own or that others can 'hear' their thoughts

Common Causes and Risk Factors for Depression

Different theories have been proposed as to why people develop clinical depression. Perhaps, the most notable among these theories are behavioral or behaviorist theory and cognitive theory.

The behaviorists think the disorder is the result of how a person responds to or interacts with their environment. But for cognitive theorists, it is more than just your behavior and environments, but also about an abnormal thinking processes.

There are several other theories that have also been suggested.

However, when talking about more specific causes, the following ones are among the most common.

Genetics

As in the cases of several other disorders, the genes you carry may be a factor in your likelihood of developing clinical depression. The disorder runs in families.

Evidence from twin and family studies suggests this, although researchers do not yet know the entire genetic risk factors.

An identical twin, for instance, is estimated to have 70 percent likelihood of also developing the condition if the other has it.

Poor Diet

You may be at risk of depression if you are the type that does not pay much attention to what you eat. Poor nutrition can deprive you of important nutrients that can help keep it at bay.

For instance, you may be at a greater risk of having this disorder if you have high amount of sugar in your diet. Low amount of omega-3 fatty acids can also make it more likely for you to suffer from it.

Brain chemical imbalance

The odds of a person having depression increase when there is an imbalance in brain chemistry. The symptoms may appear when there is a drop in the amount of key neurotransmitters.

These chemicals facilitate communication between different areas of the brain, helping to regulate mood. There is bound to be issues, including memory problems, when the levels are low.

Medical disorders

Depression may be an effect of a physical health challenge. It is common knowledge that whatever affects your body can impact your mind - the reverse is also true.

The mental illness is a symptom of certain physical health issues, including liver disease, diabetes, Addison's disease, Cushing's syndrome, and stroke.

Medical conditions can cause you to become depressed due to the stress that comes with them.

Drugs

Both prescription drugs and drugs of abuse can cause depression as a side effect. many prescription medications and drug and/or alcohol abuse is considered common in those who are depressed.

Anticonvulsants, beta-blockers, antipsychotics, and contraceptives are among the medical agents that can lead to the mood disorder. Other associated treatments include drugs for migraine, statins, hormonal agents, and interferon therapy.

It's probably even worse with substances of drugs of abuse such as alcohol, amphetamines, cocaine and heroin. These can both cause and aggravate the condition.

Life events

unfortunate life events of any individual are obvious triggers for depression. Rape, relationship problems, loss of a loved one, financial challenges, separation, and social isolation are some of the life events that can cause it.

Other risk factors include:

- Being female
- Sexuality (e.g. gay or lesbian)
- Poverty
- Circadian rhythm disturbance

It is also worth adding that the personality of some people makes them more prone to being depressed. people who tend to be pessimistic, have low self-esteem or are easily susceptible to stress are at a greater risk..

S.E. Charles

CHAPTER 2 - SIGNS THAT YOU MAY HAVE DEPRESSION

Now and again you might hear people talk about being depressed. That's nothing out of the ordinary. Certain life events are capable of bringing the mood of practically anyone down - talk about the loss of a loved one or of a well-paying job.

But it is not always correct to assume that anyone who is experiencing a low mood suffers from clinical depression, also known as major depressive disorder.

For a person to be diagnosed with the mental illness, such must have exhibited certain symptoms for at least a specific length of time. We discuss here some possible warning signs of clinical depression as well as how you can better know whether you have it.

Signs that You Possibly Have Depression

Clinical depression can have profound negative impact

on an individual, their family, and relationships. It presents symptoms that put those affected at significant risk of debilitating medical conditions and death.

Let's consider some of symptoms it may present.

Anxiety

Depression and anxiety go together. When one is being talked about, it is highly likely the other would be mentioned as well. They are practically inseparable.

So, you may suspect depression if you notice that you are becoming more anxious about situations than ever. It's not really that one causes the other; they are just related.

Rapid heartbeat, fast breathing, panic attacks, nervousness, and increased perspiration are among symptoms of anxiety.

According to the 1990-92 National Comorbidity Survey in the United States, about 50 percent of persons with major depressive disorder have lifetime anxiety as well.

Sleep problems and fatigue

Depression can throw your sleep cycle or routine out of order. Insomnia is a common occurrence among people having it. These individuals often wake earlier than normal or ideal and find it difficult going back to sleep.

When you don't sleep well, you may not have enough energy to go through your day. It can cause you to experience extreme fatigue.

The disorder may also dispose you to hypersomnia, or excessive sleep. This effect may be encouraged by feeling of crushing fatigue.

Loss of interest or pleasure

The low mood seen in depression pervades every aspect of a person's life. It is so serious to cause you not to derive pleasure anymore in activities you enjoyed in the past.

It could even make people who are ordinarily excited by opportunity for sexual activity to lose interest in it. Men may have erection problems as a result.

Hopelessness and worthlessness

People experiencing depression commonly feel very hopeless. You may even see some asking whether there is anything worth living for.

You probably have the disorder if you often find yourself occupied with thoughts of worthlessness, helplessness, inappropriate guilt or self-hatred.

Irritability

Depression can cause some people to become irritable. For instance, children with the mental illness have been found to become more irritable than depressed.

Researchers have also found that irritability is one of the symptoms that depressed men may exhibit.

Appetite changes

This illness can cause your eating pattern to change in somewhat unpredictable manner.

More commonly, depression causes a person to lose appetite, thereby leading to weight loss. But it can also bring about increased appetite and weight gain in some instances.

A clue to tell whether appetite changes are worth worrying about is to assess whether they are intentional or otherwise.

Other symptoms you may observe include:

Restlessness
Concentration problems
Problem with decision making
Difficulty remembering things
Constant headaches
Persistent cramps
Digestive issues

It has been found that depression also causes mood swings. One moment you may see a person having it laughing and they start crying the next.

Severe cases could cause people to have delusions or hallucinations - believing or seeing what is not real or existing.

Another extreme symptom of the disorder are suicidal thoughts. An affected individual may constantly have the thoughts of putting an end to their own lives.

How is Depression Diagnosed?

A well-trained and qualified professional is in the best position to help tell whether what you are feeling is depression or not. This could be your regular family doctor, a psychiatrist, or a psychologist.

There is actually no specific test that can show at once if you are having clinical depression. It takes a combination of techniques to diagnose it.

Usually, diagnosis will start with an examination of your history - biographical, family and/or medical. A physical examination will also be performed. The first aim here is to assess how biological, psychological, social and environmental factors may be contributing.

You should expect to be asked about the symptoms that you have noticed - both past and current. Your health professional will inquire about the severity and how long you have been seeing symptoms. They may ask about how you manage them, to know whether this includes use of substances.

There will also be an examination to ascertain your mental state. This can help to assess how your thought process may be worsening the condition.

Tools used for mental examination include the Beck Depression Inventory and the Hamilton Rating Scale for Depression. Although the reliance on a rating scale makes these inadequate singly for diagnosis, they can serve as pointers of severity.

A number of other tests will usually also be done to rule out other conditions, such as vitamin D deficiency, hypothyroidism, hypogonadism, or systemic infections. A CT scan may also be necessary to rule out brain pathology.

Researchers have also identified certain biomarkers that may serve as pointers to depression. One of such is brain-derived neurotrophic factor (BDNF).

When to Get Help

Knowing when to seek the help of a professional can be the difference between well-being and tragedy.

Seek professional assistance as soon as possible if you observe two or more of the depressive symptoms lasting for two weeks or more.

It is particularly advisable that you consider getting help if you observe the symptoms getting in the way of important things in your life. You should do that when they start causing work, study or relationship problems.

Do not delay a minute longer before contacting your health professional for help if you notice suicidal thoughts. Mood swings and increased appetite for risks that may result in death are among the warning signs.

Watch out when someone you know and who has depression starts making comments bordering on how helpless, worthless or hopeless they feel. Also, pay careful attention when such often talks about things related to death or suicide. They may be contemplating ending it all.

Get help right immediately you notice yourself or someone you know having suicidal thoughts. Either reach out to your mental health professional at once or put a call through to the suicide hotline in your area.

That may be the best decision you'll ever make.

The good news is that depression is not something you can absolutely nothing about. It is a treatable condition.

Your mental health professional will guide you on the different options that are available for managing the disorder. As in the case of anxiety, medications and psychotherapy are the main approaches for treatment.

You can also get help in improving the symptoms of depression by making certain lifestyle changes. Your doctor will be able to guide you more on those.

S.E. Charles

CHAPTER 3 - TREATMENT OPTIONS FOR DEPRESSION

Depression is a mental illness capable of making a person's life a nightmare. Thankfully, there are different treatment options available to fight it.

The best approach to use for treating depression usually depends on its type and severity. Often, it takes more than one method to effectively deal with the illness.

Here are the different treatment options available for depression

Medicinal Treatment for Depression

The use of medications is arguably the most popular means of dealing with depression. These drugs are known as antidepressants. They rank among the most used medicines in the United States.

There are different types of antidepressant medications that may be taken to deal with this disorder. These work mainly by helping to balance brain chemistry. They produce effects on three major brain chemicals, namely: serotonin, norepinephrine, and dopamine.

We discuss the most popular of these drugs below.

Selective serotonin reuptake inhibitors (SSRIs)

It is not uncommon for doctors to first recommend this when it comes to drugs for depression. SSRIs are the most prescribed type of antidepressants. The drugs help to improve how circuits in your brain use serotonin.

Selective serotonin reuptake inhibitors are more popular because they usually have fewer side effects. Examples of these drugs include sertraline (Zoloft), citapolam (Celexa), and fluoxetine (Prozac).

Serotonin and norepinephrine reuptake inhibitors (SNRIs)

These medications help to improve your mood by producing effects on brain circuits that utilize serotonin and norepinephrine. Among those used for treating depression are duloxetine (Cymbalta), Desvenlafaxine (Pristiq), and venlafaxine (Effexor XR).

Research suggests that venlafaxine may be slightly more effective than SSRIs. The main concern is that it may come with more side effects.

Tricyclic antidepressants (TCAs)

Also known as cyclic antidepressants, TCAs are an older variant of antidepressants. They work mainly by helping to boost both serotonin and norepinephrine levels in the brain, similar to SNRIs.

But they are no longer as popular because they produce

more side effects. Doctors will usually try an SSRI on a patient first before considering a tricyclic antidepressant.

Examples of TCAs include amitriptyline (Amitid, Elavil) and imipramine (Tofranil).

Monoamine oxidase inhibitors (MAOIs)

As in the case of TCAs, MAOIs may be suggested only after trying out other types of drugs for depression. They were the first type of these drugs, but they are now less used because of their potential for serious side effects.

Utmost care is important when using a MAOI. You'd usually be asked to maintain a rather severe diet. The drugs can have hazardous interactions with certain foods, including wine and cheese. They also interact with some other medications and supplements. You cannot use them with the safer SSRIs.

Examples of monoamine oxidase inhibitors include isocarboxazid (Marplan), selegiline (Emsam), and phenelzine (Nardil). Selegiline, available as a skin patch, is a newer variant with fewer side effects.

Atypical antidepressants

These are drugs that help with depression but do not fall clearly into any of the categories of antidepressants. Among them are bupropion (Wellbutrin), vortioxetine (Trintellix), and mirtazapine (Remeron).

In addition to the above drugs, your doctor may also put you on anti-anxiety medications and stimulants. Antipsychotics may also come into the picture.

Two types of antidepressants may be used together or combined with other drugs, such as those for bipolar disorder or schizophrenia.

Psychotherapy for Depression

The fact that antidepressants are very popularly used for treatment doesn't make them more effective. Some experts argue that psychotherapy, or talk therapy, may be the best first-line intervention. This is especially so for mild to moderate cases.

The use of medications comes with risk of many side effects. These adverse reactions may be hard to justify in some cases of the disorder.

Psychotherapy is particularly ideal for younger people, mainly those below the age of 18. It has been found that the use of antidepressants increases the risk of suicidal thoughts or behaviors in persons younger than 25 years.

So what's psychotherapy about?

This is an approach to treatment that involves you talking with a mental health professional about the disorder and related issues. The aim here is to improve your mindset and convey skills that can help you deal with issues that may come with the disorder.

There are various types of psychotherapy that can be used for the treatment of depression. Among the most common or popular ones are cognitive behavioral therapy, psychodynamic therapy and interpersonal therapy.

Your treatment program may involve a combination of different therapies.

With psychotherapy, you get to learn ways by which you can deal with negative thinking. It helps you to know the underlying causes of the disorder as well as the triggers and reasons you feel a particular way. Therapy can be helpful for setting realistic goals and having a sense of satisfaction in your life.

Talk therapy is not necessarily something you undergo alone. Your mental health professional may suggest having it with your family or in a group, depending on the degree.

Group therapy may especially be beneficial for faster recovery. It makes you know you are not alone in the struggle, while learning from experiences of others.

Other Treatment Options

Medications and psychotherapy are the two major means of treating depression. But there are a number of other options available besides them.

Electroconvulsive therapy (ECT) – This will more likely be considered only if you do not respond to other types of treatment. ECT is often used when a patient is thought capable of causing harm to self or others and other treatment options are considered ineffective or too slow to prevent that.

Also known as electroshock therapy, this involves transmission of electric currents through your brain via the scalp. The currents impact the neurotransmitters in the brain, helping to improve their function.

Transcranial magnetic stimulation (TMS) – Patients who haven't responded to medical treatment for depression are the ideal candidates for this therapy.

It entails placing an electromagnetic treatment coil against your scalp. This emits magnetic pulses that cause stimulation of nerve cells in the brain. TMS specifically impacts the prefrontal cortex, which is involved in mood regulation.

This treatment isn't as effective as ECT. You would need to undergo it several times a week for up to about a month and half.

Vagus nerve stimulation – This is more of a surgical procedure and it is reserved for people whose condition has defied other forms of interventions.

Vagus nerve stimulation involves implantation of a device that looks like a pacemaker in your chest. This frequently sends electric currents to the vagus nerve in your neck via wires. Researchers think that this produces effects on brain region associated to depression.

It may take several months to notice any improvement.

Knowing Your Options

Treatment of depression usual involves combination of the different options available. Faster recovery is possible when you also make certain important lifestyle changes.

Antidepressants are very popular when it comes to treatment of depression. But these can produce serious side events, including increasing risk of suicidal thoughts or behaviors. They are also not ideal for pregnant or nursing mother.

It is obviously crucial to only use antidepressants if your doctor recommends any to you. It might take a bit of trial and error to find what will work for you. Make sure that you use these drugs as advised. Do not stop taking them before speaking with your health professional because that may bring serious issues.

Psychotherapy is a safer approach to treatment of

depression. You may be able to improve faster when you combine it with medication use. You can continue with it for as long as you wish without safety issues, unlike in the case of antidepressants.

S.E. Charles

CHAPTER 4- LIFESTYLE CHANGES FOR MANAGING YOUR DEPRESSION

Depression can be a big burden to carry. How unpleasant it could be to find that somehow you no longer enjoy your favorite activities and life doesn't seem exciting anymore. That's actually depressing!

In previous chapters, we covered the different types of drugs that help battle the disorder and help get your life back. There is also psychotherapy for more effective recovery.

Sometimes, however, psychotherapy and medications may not be enough for effective treatment. If you have reached that point where these don't seem to help much, you need to consider changing your lifestyle. It is still helpful to make changes, even if you haven't gotten to that point yet.

Lifestyle changes don't demand too much from you and, yet, can be powerful means of treatment. In this chapter… we provide some tips that may make all the difference for you.

Lose Excess Fat

It is helpful to consider shedding some pounds if you happen to be overweight or obese. Weight loss is well known to be a way to enjoy great health. It keeps many health issues at bay.

But you may ask: how exactly does it help with depression? It helps mainly by making you feel good about yourself.

People with anxiety and depression issues are believed to often have poor body image. They feel that they are not perfect for a reason or another. Being overweight or obese may be one of the seeming "imperfections."

Therefore, by losing weight, your self-esteem can improve. This, in turn, can help reduce your depression.

Have a Regular Exercise Schedule

This is one of two main ways of enjoying great health – the other being a healthy diet. Exercise can help with this disorder due to how it boosts natural antidepressants in your body.

It causes your body to produce more neurotransmitters, especially endorphins and serotonin. These brain chemicals are crucial for mood regulation. They are the "feel good" factors. They are the reason people report being "happy" after exercising.

Another thing about exercise that makes it beneficial is that it helps you have a great body. It boosts your confidence and raises your self-esteem. You can also find it beneficial in making social connections.

All these benefits make exercise perfect for anyone

with depression.

It doesn't have to be anything very strenuous, really. You can feel better from even walking for just about 30 minutes daily.

Eat Well

Now, by eating well, is not a reference to ensuring your stomach is filled. Rather, you need to ensure you only consume healthy foods. Keep away from all the junks.

Experts advise that diets rich in healthy fatty acids, such as Omega-3, can be quite useful to people with depression. You can get these fatty acids from foods such as fish, olive oil and nuts.

But eating healthily for depression management doesn't mean being on some restrictive diet.

You just need to eat lots of vegetables, fruits, and whole grains, according to WebMD. Monitor your calorie intake and reduce the amount of sugar in your diet. In addition, avoid foods or drinks that contain caffeine as much as possible.

Enjoy the Sunlight

These days, many people go to great lengths to avoid the sun or protect themselves against it. You want to think twice about doing that as someone dealing with depression.

Sunlight is good for boosting the mood. You are at a greater risk of feeling down if you get too little. This explains why depression is more common during winter months and in places with minimal sunlight.

You want to ensure you get more sunlight then. Your doctor may be able to help with light therapy, if there is less sunlight in your area.

De-stress

Effective stress management is one of the things to include in your lifestyle changes. Determine what causes you stress to see how you can deal with the triggers.

Make conscious efforts to relax. This might mean setting aside a specific period each day for relaxation. Keep aside all work and do all you can to let off the steam.

Relaxation can mean different things to different people. For some, it is reading a book, while it is watching a movie for another. It may mean mediation or yoga for still some other people.

Determine what healthy way helps you relax the most and indulge in it.

Get Restful Sleep

Sleep is an aspect that also suffers in the presence of depression. You find it hard to get quality bedtime each night. Thoughts raging in your head make things difficult. You might wake up in the middle of the night and find it impossible getting back to sleep.

Yet, you need to sleep well to be more effective in dealing with the symptoms. You become easily tired when this is lacking. This can further aggravate the symptoms.

Sleep helps to replenish brain chemicals that play a role in the regulation of your mood. Researchers have observed that people who fail to get quality bedtime are at a very great risk of developing depression.

It will help to have a regular schedule. Try to go to bed and get up at about the same time every day. Cut screen staring well before going to sleep. You may do something relaxing, such as reading a book, to put you in the mood.

Keep Away from Alcohol and Drugs

If you drink, you should consider limiting the amount for the sake of improving your depression. It is actually best that you quit drinking completely. But that might seem too hard, so consider lowering your alcohol consumption instead if you can't.

Some people turn to alcohol and other drugs as a way of lifting their moods. But they are really courting trouble by so doing.

Research shows strong connection between substance abuse and depression.

When their effects wear away, alcohol and other drugs can leave you worse off than you were before taking them. Continual use further compounds the problem. therefore, it's best to keep away from them.

Have Support

It helps to have people around or that you can look to for help in managing your depression.

There is often that tendency for someone with depression to want to stay away from people. No, you need to guard against that!

You should attempt to establish and maintain strong social relationships. This will be useful as something to fall back on when you are beginning to feel down.

In addition to your family and friends, you can also think about joining a club or group. Take a class. Volunteer. Having a pet nearby can even by helpful.

Connection with the right people – caring and

supportive – will be of great value to you. It can help steer clear of isolation and loneliness, which usually encourage the disorder.

Smile More

This might sound rather odd. How do you ask a depressed person to smile more? That's a little like asking someone to give what he doesn't have.

Professor Jane A. Plant, who thinks people with depression need to give more thoughts to lifestyle changes than medical treatments, told Psych Central that patients can feel better by smiling.

The professor of geochemistry at the Imperial College London argues that this is a great way of making your brain think everything is alright, even when it isn't. Smiling can improve people's reaction towards you and that may help you feel better by boosting your mood.

What You Should Know

These lifestyle changes, and others you may find, can go a long way in enhancing your recovery. They can enhance the effectiveness of other treatment options.

However, these changes may appear easier said than done, especially for someone facing depression. They might be hard to do but not entirely impossible.

It may not be realistic to make these changes all at once. It is actually not advisable doing that because you will most likely fail. The key thing is to start somewhere and progress from there.

CHAPTER 5 – HOW EXERCISE HELPS WITH DEPRESSION

Regular exercise is one of those lifestyle changes that are often recommended for faster recovery from depression. However, this is not something many people with the disorder will find interesting enough to do.

But studies show that this is something you will need to do all the same to regain control of your mental health. Perhaps, having an idea of how exercise can be helpful can get you motivated. find out how it helps in this chapter.

Connection Between Physical and Mental Health

It is not hard to understand that mental health has a connection to physical health. For instance, when your body feels tired, your brain is not likely to perform at its best. That's probably how simply we can describe this connection.

Why the reason is not entirely clear, experts know that there is a link between your physical state and your mental health. Your psychological functions improve with exercise. Research suggests that physical activity can help ease depression.

It has been found that people who are physically active are at a lower risk of having anxiety or depression than those who maintain an inactive lifestyle.

Researchers observed in one study that people who engaged in vigorous exercise regularly have about 25 percent lower risk of developing depression or an anxiety disorder in the following five years.

A review of medical studies by Harvard Medical School showed that exercise can be beneficial to people with mild or moderate depression.

Moderate exercise – in terms of intensity – done five days a week was found to reduce symptoms by almost half after 12 weeks in a study done by researchers at the Southwestern Medical Center of the University of Texas.

How Does it Help?

There are several ways by which exercise may help you feel better from depression. Let's consider some of the most important.

Brain chemical effect

Depression inhibits the effects of chemicals in the brain, making communication between areas of the organ difficult. It makes it difficult to respond appropriately to situations.

Exercise can help to solve the problem, partly by improving the release of neurotransmitters. It stimulates the sympathetic nervous system to promote release of important chemicals, such as serotonin, norepinephrine, and dopamine.

Physical activity improves the production of brain-derived neurotrophic factor (BDNF). This protein makes it easier for neurotransmitters to do their job.

You get greater amount of the feel-good endorphins when you exercise. The endogenous opioid substances influence nerve cell response to neurotransmitters. They lessen pain, anxiety and depression. The chemicals help to fight stress and improve your mood, possibly even making you joyful.

Promotion of neurogenesis

Another way exercise can help with depression is by promoting new nerve cell growth. This is what neurogenesis means. This effect has to do with the boost in BDNF levels mentioned earlier.

When you sweat from exercising, the protein FNDC5 is released into the bloodstream, according to Psych Central. It is this that stimulates BDNF, which, in turn, protects existing cells while also stimulating growth of new nerve cells and synapses.

This benefit is especially important to older people. It is believed that people start to lose nerve cells from their 30s.

Useful distraction

People with depression or anxiety can also benefit from exercise due to how it helps to take their minds of their worries – at least, for a short while. It makes you break free from the seemingly never-ending negative thoughts.

You may find it easier getting distracted, in a good way, when you do physical activity outdoors. This also enables you enjoy sunlight, which is known for its ability to boost mood.

In addition to the above benefits, exercise can help boost your self-confidence and self-esteem. You may succeed in making new, useful social connections while at it as well.

Exercise is by far a better means of dealing with depression than other things sufferers often resort to. It is beneficial for good health, unlike habits such as drug and alcohol use.

Starting an Exercise Program

With all the benefits it offers, you can obviously see why it will be beneficial to include physical activity into your regular schedule. You should consider planning and starting an exercise program to enjoy these benefits.

When talking about an exercise program, this doesn't necessarily have to be something cast in stone or strict. An important consideration when it comes to increasing activity level to fight depression is pleasure.

It is not a must that you do highly intensive strength or endurance training, although that may be more beneficial. If something you find enjoyable is less strenuous, you can start with that in the meantime. This might be walking, jogging, running, swimming, or even gardening.

You should adopt a gradual approach to your exercise program. It may not be advisable to aim attaining a particular goal at once.

For instance, if the recommendation is for you to exercise daily, it might initially be difficult to adjust to this. You may start with alternate days. You can then make it an everyday affair as you get used to the routine.

It is helpful to only do your exercise in a setting that makes you comfortable. It is beneficial if such can enable you to work out without losing interest.

There is advantage to getting active in places where you have other people exercising. Seeing these other persons might serve as encouragement.

You may also choose to do your exercise at home if you tend to be uncomfortable in company of others. But still, there is more to benefit from having someone to work with. Consider finding a friend who enjoys similar physical activities as you.

How Much Exercise Do You Need?

You should aim at exercising for at least 30 minutes a day, 3-5 days a week, to see significant improvement in your depression symptoms, according to Mayo Clinic.

However, if you are reluctant to spend that much time, you can start with shorter time. It will be better than doing nothing at all.

You can still see improvement in symptoms when you exercise for about 10-15 minutes each day. In fact, some mental health researchers say that there isn't much separating the level of relief you get from a 10-minute walk and a 45-minute workout.

It gets even better if you can make your exercise vigorous for the short duration. This requires less time to boost your mood and the effect can last for hours.

A Word of Caution

Research has shown that exercise can be as effective as drugs for treatment of depression in some people. But that's not to say it is an alternative to medications. It only makes a crucial inclusion for faster recovery.

Therefore, you should continue using whatever

antidepressants your doctor prescribes, especially when they don't produce nasty side effects. Do not stop your psychotherapy sessions also.

It is worthy to consider consulting to your doctor to first before starting any exercise program. This will help to ensure that you won't be aggravating some other health conditions.

A medical expert can help in determining what form of exercise will be suitable as well as the ideal level of intensity. You may also get tips for staying motivated from such.

Finally, we should mention that you should be prepared for setbacks when doing exercise for depression relief. There may be time you may feel like not continuing with the program. This is a major reason it helps to have a partner.

If you happen to fail to exercise on any day, you can try again the following day. Do not feel discouraged if progress seems too slow – it's still progress all the same.

S.E. Charles

CHAPTER 6 – HELPING A FRIEND OR FAMILY MEMBER WITH DEPRESSION

Its heart wrenching seeing a loved one battling with depression. You want to help them, but you are just not sure how to go about doing so. You are careful about doing something that might worsen their condition.

The fact that you are concerned about the wellbeing of a friend or family member having this mental disorder is a good thing. That simply shows you are the kind of person they need around. As to how you can help them, we provide some tips you can work with in this chapter.

Learn all you can

When seeking to help a friend or family member with depression, it is not wise to just assume you know what the disorder is about. Unless you have experienced something similar in the past.

It is important to learn as much as you can about the illness. This will be useful in having the right perspective about it, so that you don't misjudge its potential severity.

Seek to understand the symptoms, which may vary

between individuals. Depression can affect your loved one in a way they seem too helpless to do anything about. It makes them to lose interest in things and people they previously loved. It's not them; they just can't help it.

Know that the symptoms of the disorder are not personal at all. When you learn more about these, you will be in a better position to be helpful.

Watch what you say

A major reason it is important to first understand depression and its symptoms is so that you know how to react. This can be useful in helping you know what to say to your loved one having the problem.

Experts advise against statements such as "it's all in your head" or "snap out of it." These could have unintended effect.

By saying such things, you might only succeed in making your friend or family member feel they are the architect of their own problem. It suggests you think it is their personal decision to feel depressed.

How insensitive that can be! This will most likely only cause them to sink deeper into isolation, worsening the disorder.

Don't assume the role of a pro

These days its pretty easy to find suggestions on what people can do to "fix" their Problems. You may feel inclined to suggest these fixes to your loved one.

Well... the truth is you are not in the right position to fix your friend or family member's problem. The only exception, perhaps, is if you are a trained mental health professional or have had similar experience yourself. You may go ahead, then, if you can manage to be less direct.

A key reason for this is to prevent making your loved one feel worse. Who knows, they might feel insulted and pull away from you.

The affected person should be the one to fix the problem, not you. The most you can do is to make yourself available to them. Ask them how you can be of help.

Give a listening ear

Helping a friend or family member with depression also demands good listening skills. You should learn to listen more than talk.

People affected by this disorder tend to keep their thoughts to themselves. So if that somewhat rare opportunity of them wanting to talk comes, ensure you make the most of it by listening with interest. It can be relieving to them to find there is someone they can always talk to without being judged.

Again, you should try to always make them realize that they can always come to you. Repeat often that you are there to help and they only need to tell you how you can help.

Lend a helping hand

One of the hallmarks of depression is finding everyday tasks too difficult to handle. You can help your loved one by asking what tasks they need help with. If you know their regular schedule, this should be easy.

Try to help with cleaning, groceries, and driving or anything you know they need. You can also offer to engage in activities they used to enjoy doing with them.

Support to seek treatment

There is limit to what you can do to help a friend or family member with depression. You are less likely to be able to do this successfully on your own. It will be beneficial to encourage them to seek treatment from a mental health professional.

There's usually less motivation to get things done when experiencing depression. This is why you should consider persuading them to take this step. However, they need to realize, or be made to, that there is a problem begging for solution.

Offer to help arrange an appointment with a mental health professional. If that doesn't sound great to them, you may suggest a routine check-up with a regular doctor. The latter option might make them more open to the idea of getting help.

You could try going with them when visiting a health professional. And when they start treatment, help them in whatever ways they need it to make the process a success. Make an effort to maintain an upbeat attitude to serve as a form of encouragement to your loved one.

Look out for signs of suicide

Among the scary things about depression is the potential to incite suicidal thoughts or behaviors. The risk of suicide is real during episodes of major depressive disorder.

It might be hard to imagine your loved one taking such a decision, but the illness can make them lose control. It distorts the natural, rational thinking process.

You can help by looking out for signs that suggest likelihood of suicide. These include expression of self-hatred or hopelessness and frequent talk about suicide or death.

Don't hesitate in reaching emergency services as soon

as you notice signs suggestive of suicidal thoughts. Monitor them while waiting for help to arrive.

Look after yourself

It is not impossible to lose sight of your own health, both physical and mental, when helping a friend of family member with depression. You may find the experience rather exhausting and frustrating.

You need to watch the extent to which you push yourself in trying to help. This will be crucial in ensuring that you don't end up needing medical attention soon. By not sacrificing your own health, you are more likely to be there for longer to be more helpful.

Do all you can to stay healthy. Eat well, get regular exercise, and ensure you do not skimp on sleep.

You might want to bring someone else on board to make it easier helping your loved one to full recovery. The other person takes over when you need to let off some steam and relax your nerves.

It's not only people with depression that have support groups. There are also groups for those taking care of them. Try to find one around your area and join.

You don't necessarily have to talk about your friend or family member in these groups, but rather discuss your own feelings. It is possible to learn a thing or two from others' experience.

It doesn't have to be strictly a support group. You can also share your feelings with a trusted friend. You can seek help from a counselor or therapist as well.

S.E. Charles

CHAPTER 7 – ALTERNATIVE TREATMENTS AND REMEDIES FOR DEPRESSION

There are several approved drugs for the treatment of depression. But there are people with the disorder who would prefer a non-drug approach to treatment. This is due to the side effects that may accompany the use of medications.

If you happen to be one of those people. There are many natural, non-drug remedies that may help with the disorder. While not all of these are truly helpful, some have been proven to help.

In this lesson well learn about the alternative treatments and remedies that can help people with depression. Some have actually been used for centuries due to their ability to improve mood.

Herbs and Supplements

There is no shortage of herbs and supplements that are marketed to be helpful for battling mental disorders, including depression. Some of them don't always help.

We discuss below some of those that have been observed to help people with depression.

St. John's wort

Although the Food and Drug Administration has yet to approve this herb for the illness, there is evidence that it may be helpful. This is especially true in mild to moderate cases.

The plant, which is native to Europe, is widely used across the continent for boosting mood. It is approved for treating depression in Germany. The popularity appears to also now be on the rise in the United States.

It was reported in the British Medicine Journal in 2005 that researchers found in a large trial that the efficacy is at least on par with a popular antidepressant.

A review of 29 trials by Cochrane researchers in 2008 also revealed that St. John's wort was as effective as antidepressants for treating the depression. In addition to the effectiveness, the herb had fewer side effects.

It is believed that the plant works by boosting in the brain levels of serotonin, which people with depression have a low amount of. It is this same way that some antidepressants also help.

Omega-3 fatty acids

It would me unlikely for you not to have heard some awesome benefit associated with omega-3 fatty acids. It is popular for promoting heart health. It can also help in fighting depression as well.

Researchers have found that two types of these compounds – docosahexaenoic acid (DHA) and eicosapentaeoic acid (EPA) – have connection to depression. People with low amounts of these fatty acids may be at a greater risk of the disorder.

A higher amount of DHA relative to EPA is thought to be better for preserving mental health.

You can get omega-3 fatty acids from fish, beans, olive oil and walnuts, among other natural sources. They are available as supplements as well.

S-Adenosyl methionine (SAM-e or SAMe)

Evidence suggests that this supplement may help improve symptoms of depression, at least in the short term. SAMe is more of a synthetic variant of chemicals in the brain that boost mood. But it is not usually regarded as a drug.

It was reported in a 2005 review of studies that patients who took the compound showed considerable improvement in their symptoms, compared to those on a placebo.

If you wish to try this supplement, it helps to go for one having enteric coating.

There are a number of other herbs and natural supplements that may also help. They include saffron, turmeric and, to a lower extent, Ginkgo biloba.

Vitamins and minerals, such as folic acid, vitamin B12, and magnesium, may also be beneficial. People who have low levels of these appear to be at a higher risk of depression.

Acupuncture

Recent research suggests that this ancient Chinese practice of healing may be at least as helpful as conventional treatment for this condition after a few months. It may especially be beneficial to people who also experience pain at the same time.

The therapy involves sticking thin needles into certain points on the body, depending on the disorder or illness. The aim is to correct imbalances in the body and so enhance its ability to fight illnesses and promote healing.

Acupuncture can also stimulate release of chemicals that reduce pain sensation and make you feel well. It is proven to help with back pain, muscle ache, headaches, and menstrual cramps.

This is arguably the best option for people whose symptoms include pain.

Massage

This offers a great way of calming your nerves and dealing with stress. As you may know, the latter is a factor in the incidence of anxiety and depression.

This systematic manipulation of the body's soft tissues and muscles can help to boost your mood. It promotes relaxation and improves circulation.

Massage helps to combat stress by leading to a drop in cortisol levels. On the other hand, it stimulates brain chemicals such as serotonin and dopamine.

There are different forms that may help promote relaxation and enhance the mind-body connection. Particularly helpful ones include Swedish massage and Reiki massage. Some forms integrate the use of essential oils to enhance the effect.

Meditation

In this therapy, you have a means of staying in control of your mind or thought processes. Meditation can help you have a better understanding of your mind. It is a good and effective way of moving from a negative mindset to positive.

Meditation is basically a form of relaxation. It involves you focusing your mind on one thing while keeping your body at rest, but awake. That one thing may be anything from a word to some imaginary place that is not linked to your depression.

Researchers have found that it can help deal with both anxiety and depression when done regularly. You need to devote as little as 10 minutes to this each day. There is more to gain when you do it for a longer length of time, though.

Yoga

This is another trending approach to dealing stress that may aggravate depression. In its real form, yoga blends spiritual, physical and mental exercises aimed at promoting overall wellbeing. The practice, which started in ancient India, often involves meditation.

It can help control symptoms suggestive of anxiety or depression, such as rapid heart rate, shallow breathing, and elevated blood pressure.

The breathing techniques help you stay calm while also capable of making you more lively when in low mood. As for the movements, they can be useful for improving your posture and making you more confident.

It was found in a study that hatha yoga, which involves

significant physical activity, was more beneficial for depression than merely education the patients on what to do. And the benefits were long-term.

Guided imagery

Here is a mind-body therapy that bears some semblance to meditation. The main aims are to lessen tension and reduce stress. Guided imagery helps to improve your mindset and to help you find it easier coping in difficult situations.

Also known as guided therapeutic imagery or guided affective imagery, this intervention involves attempt by a trained practitioner to help you create calming mental images. These serve as an escape from troubling thoughts. The process may involve use of audiovisual materials.

An example of images you may create is a beautiful, scenic beach. Practically anything or place that makes you feel relaxed may be evoked.

Guided imagery is a powerful coping tool. It not only helps with depression, but also several other issues, including insomnia and pain.

In addition to the above-mentioned, some may also consider exercise as an alternative form of treatment. This indeed works, but it is more of a change in lifestyle.

These alternative treatments and remedies for depression are not necessarily alternatives to medications or psychotherapy. We advise that you speak with your doctor before opting for any of them.

Some of the herbs and supplements may interact with drugs you may already be taking, including antidepressants. Speaking with a medical professional will help ensure you are making an indeed wise decision.

Please Leave a Review

Finally, if you enjoyed this book, please take the time to share your thoughts and post a review. It'd be greatly appreciated!

That review and feedback will help me improve the content in my books – and make each and every one more relevant and helpful to you.

Thank you again and good luck!

S.E. Charles

Preview of 'Cognitive Behavioral Therapy: A CBT Beginners Guide to Defeating Anxiety, Depression, Phobias and Low-Self Esteem' by S.E. Charles

Chapter 1 - Understanding the Fundamentals

Cognitive behavioral therapy (CBT) is a form of talk therapy or psychotherapy that aims to help patients manage or control problems by altering how they think and behavior. It offers a practical approach to dealing with issues.

The treatment combines the principles of both behavioral and cognitive psychology. It helps with a wide range of mental health challenges.

History of Cognitive Behavioral Therapy

Certain aspects of this form of psychotherapy have been traced back to ancient times. They are believed to have link to some ancient philosophical traditions, especially Stoicism.

Epictetus and some other Stoic philosophers thought that false beliefs that brought about unhelpful emotions can be identified and dealt with through the use of logic. Such views provided foundation for modern cognitive-behavioral theories.

The origin of CBT as we now know it is traced to the early 20th century when behavior therapy emerged. Cognitive therapy was developed in the 1960s. The two therapies were reportedly combined by psychiatrist Aaron Beck in the 1960s, leading to emergence of cognitive behavioral therapy.

The psychotherapy form was originally used for treatment of depression. While cognitive therapy is only a part of it, CBT is now often seen as incorporating all forms of cognitive-based psychotherapies.

Some Assumptions of Cognitive Behavioral Therapy

The aim with CBT is to improve the awareness of a patient when he or she is interpreting things or situations wrongly. It teaches them to be more aware of certain behaviors that can add force to negative thoughts.

A number of assumptions are involved in this treatment. They include:

A disorder is the result of poor or wrong perception about oneself, other people, or the world. This may be caused by cognitive distortions (too much emphasis on negatives and less on positives).
How a person views the world conditions how he or she interacts with it. There may be disordered thoughts and behaviors when this mental representation of the world is faulty.

Symptoms of an issue can be improved by showing patients how to cope and equipping them with skills that enable them to process information rightly.
Cognitive behavioral therapy, therefore, seeks to correct cognitive distortions. It aims to fix erroneous perception and the magnification of negatives. It helps patients to see things more for what they truly are.

CBT Uses

Cognitive behavioral therapy is almost exclusively used for treatment of disorders that has connection to mental health. It has been shown to be effective for the following disorders, among others.

Anxiety disorders

There is evidence that people suffering from anxiety disorders, especially adults, can benefit from undergoing CBT. One of the techniques that therapists use for combating anxiety is exposure. The idea behind this is that people may get to unlearn fear by being exposed to the stimulus responsible for their fears.

For instance, a person who gets anxious when in a public setting may be encouraged to give a speech in front of an audience.

Eating Disorders

It is believed that cognitive behavioral therapy may be more effective for combating eating disorders. This is in comparison to the use of medications or dependence on regular talk therapy alone.

This is actually the first-line intervention for bulimia nervosa and non-specific eating disorders. Therapists can help patients to learn how to control unhelpful behaviors and avoid negative self-image and its effects.

Depression

Treatment of this disorder was one of the first uses of cognitive behavioral therapy. There is significant evidence that it is helpful for clinical depression. The therapy helps to correct the bias towards negative thoughts in depressed individuals.

Along with interpersonal psychotherapy, it is the treatment that is most efficacious for major depressive disorder, according to the American Psychiatric Association Practice Guidelines (April 2000).

Other issues that cognitive behavioral therapy may help with include:

- Psychosis
- Schizophrenia
- Smoking
- Gambling addiction
- Chronic low back pain
- Panic attacks
- Phobias
- Anger
- Chronic fatigue syndrome
- Substance abuse
- Obsessive-compulsive disorder
- Suicidal behaviors

However, people who tend to benefit the most are those who realize they have a problem that needs to be dealt with and who are open to CBT concepts and requirements. This is because the therapy depends greatly on having specific goals.

Be Sure to Check out the rest of " *Cognitive Behavioral Therapy: A CBT Beginners Guide to Defeating Anxiety, Depression, Phobias and Low-Self Esteem*" where available.